CW00554518

Fr Willie Doyle & World War I

A Chaplain's Story

by
K. V. Turley

*All booklets are published thanks to the
generous support of the members of the
Catholic Truth Society*

CATHOLIC TRUTH SOCIETY
PUBLISHERS TO THE HOLY SEE

Contents

All rights reserved. First published 2014 by The Incorporated Catholic Truth Society, 40-46 Harleyford Road London SE11 5AY Tel: 020 7640 0042 Fax: 020 7640 0046. © 2014 The Incorporated Catholic Truth Society.

Inside images: Taken from *Father William Doyle S.J.*, by Alfred O'Rahilly. Out of copyright. Image page 61: *Battlefield of Passchendaele* © Hulton-Deutsch Collection/CORBIS.

ISBN 978 1 86082 906 2

Prologue

"I have told you all my escapes, dearest Father, because I think what I have written will give you the same confidence which I feel, that my old armchair up in Heaven is not ready yet, and I do not want you to be uneasy about me. I am all the better for these couple of days' rest, and am quite on my fighting legs again. Leave will be possible very shortly, I think, so I shall only say au revoir in view of an early meeting. Heaps of love to every dear one.

As ever, dearest Father, your loving son, Willie. 14/8/17."

Two days later the author of this letter was dead.

There were many left with unmarked graves during the Great War and that was the unremarkable fate of the military chaplain Father Willie Doyle. In his case, however, it was to be curiously fitting. For this Irish Jesuit had daily sought to walk the path of self-immolation, thus making the final 'act' of his life's drama, with its absence of tomb or marker, a not wholly unexpected finale. Nevertheless, that was not to be the end of the matter.

As with so many of his contemporaries, Doyle had travelled from the relative peace of the Edwardian age to the mechanised bloodstained nightmare that came to be known as the Great War. In those muddied plains, with their flooded stagnant trenches, when all around appeared to be proof of the worst of human depravity, one story, at least, emerged that had given hope to many at the Front, pointing to a very different world. At its centre, stood a man whose life was as compassionate as it had proved poignant, as selfless as it was heroic.

Superficially here was an ordinary, if much-loved, priest with a ready smile and a pronounced sense of fun. Only after his interment did a more intriguing narrative begin to emerge. Discovered after his death was a set of personal papers that he had asked to be burned. They comprised intimate notes revealing a radically intense life of prayer and penance, all with one aim: holiness, at any price.

"Leave will be possible very shortly," he wrote in that last letter from the Front; sadly, this was not to be. Instead, Passchendaele was to claim him. Yet, this seeming annihilation of just another military chaplain stands contradicted by his unexpected return to the consciousness of our times. It is as though, in spite of the decades that have since passed, his life's witness has once more arisen from those now still battlefields. And in so doing, it has become a testament, in stark contrast, even rebuke, to this age of ease and infidelity. The 'war' today may no longer be of worldly empires, but his faithful witness in the spiritual battle that we, too, still face is like a long-forgotten reveille

I have told you all my escapes, dearest Father because I think what I have written will give you the same confidence which I feel that my old arm-chair up in Heaven is not ready yet, and I do not want you to be uneasy about me. I am all the better for these couple of days' rest and am quite on my fighting legs again. Leave will be possible very shortly, I think, so I shall only say au revoir in view of an early meeting. Heaps of love to every dear one. As ever, dearest Father, Your loving son Willie 14/8/'17.

Facsimile of Father Doyle's last written words.

sounding anew its uncompromising call for nothing less than the martyrdom of self: sanctity.

"How many deceive themselves in thinking sanctity consists in the 'holy follies' of the saints! How many look upon holiness as something beyond their reach or capability, and think that it is to be found only in the performance of extraordinary actions. Satisfied that they have not the strength for great austerities, the time for much prayer, or the courage for painful humiliations, they silence their conscience with the thought that great sanctity is not for them, that they have not been called to be saints. With their eyes fixed on the heroic deeds of the few, they miss the daily little sacrifices God asks them to make; and while waiting for something great to prove their love, they lose the countless little opportunities of sanctification each day bears with it in its bosom."

The Child

Born on 3rd March 1873, William Joseph Gabriel Doyle had by all accounts a happy childhood. Raised in a well-to-do household in late Victorian County Dublin, his father, Hugh, who worked at Dublin's High Court of Justice, was part of the growing and increasingly influential Catholic middle class.

All the family, including aunts and his grandmother, lived together overlooking Dublin Bay, at Dalkey, in a large house called *Melrose*. Willie was the youngest of seven children. He was particularly close to his older brother, Charlie, who later would prove instrumental in helping determine the course of his vocation. In fact, no less than four of the seven children were to enter religious life or the priesthood. Clearly the Doyle household was devout, but it was more than that. All who came into contact with the family noticed that they appeared to incarnate the very essence of a Christian home. They were united in devotion to one another; something matched only by a love for the Faith - its practice and beliefs being their very cornerstone.

The servants of the house were as much a part of this as the family, and were treated as such, particularly by the young Willie. Equally so were the poor of the neighbourhood who became young Master Doyle's friends and whom he visited often. One story from his childhood relates how he left the house with eager anticipation, pocket money in hand, to go to a local sweet shop only to meet a beggar and to return poorer and empty-handed - such was the good nature of the boy that was to be refined further in the man. Even then, at this early stage, his was a life lived for others: his parents; brothers and sisters; the servants and the local poor. Nevertheless, Willie was still a boy and, like most young boys, had a sense of fun and adventure. Alongside his brother, Charlie, he was regularly in the thick of something or other - often misadventure - in the normal way of children. Other than the sweet disposition he demonstrated to all, he was just a normal boy.

One childhood incident, however, did seem to preface the man to come. One Lent, his mother came across Willie talking to a mirror. He was telling his reflected image of the starvation and deprivations to expect during the coming Lenten season. In this minor vignette we have the man of later life in miniature - for, as we shall see, what would emerge during the course of his life was first and foremost a penitential soul with a profound sense of the value of penance not only as reparation, but also as the means to live his Christian vocation to the full.

"One thing I ask of you, dear child: Don't be a saint by halves, but give Him all He asks and always. 'My way is sure.' I think I can say now, without a shade of doubt or hesitation that the path by which Jesus wants me to walk is that of absolute abandonment of all human comfort and pleasure and the embracing as far as I can of every discomfort and pain. Every time I see a picture of the crucifixion or a cross, I feel strangely affected and drawn to the life of immolation in a strange way. The heroism of Jesus appeals to me; His 'naked crucifixion' calls to me and it gives me great consolation and peace to offer myself to Him on the cross for this perpetual living crucifixion. How often does He not seem to say to me in prayer, 'I would have you strip yourself of all things - every tiny particle of self-indulgence, and this ever and always? Give Me all and I will make you a great saint.' This then is the price of my life-long yearning for sanctification. O Jesus, I am so weak, help me to give You all and to do it now."

The Scholar

Schooled at home until he was aged 11, he was then sent to Ratcliffe College in Leicestershire. Here he would spend six years happily playing sports and studying - in that order. For Willie was not, even by his own admission, academic. During his time there, however, some began to perceive something far more noteworthy. He had a presence, a charisma even, that marked him out from the other boys, helped no doubt by the fact that he was growing into a tall, charming young man. Popular with boys and masters alike, he was, nonetheless, just like any other adolescent, full of playfulness and innocent mischief. He was still noted as a friend to all, and as generous as ever. Many wondered what would become of this young man? Although as pious as his fellow pupils, there was nothing that immediately suggested a religious vocation, at least to the Rosminian priests that taught him. Here again we glimpse another of the traits that were to characterise the later life of the, by then, Father Willie Doyle. To those closest to him, his parents for example, it was clear that the young Willie would become a priest; however, to the world around him, including his teachers, this was still unclear. Years later, after having indeed become a priest, the true extent of how he entered into that state was, as before, to be revealed rarely, and only to those with eyes to see.

"A want of will is the chief obstacle to our becoming saints. We are not holy because we do not really wish to become so. We would indeed gladly possess the virtues of the saints - their humility and patience, their love of suffering, their penance and zeal. But we are unwilling to embrace all that goes to make a saint and to enter on the narrow path which leads to sanctity. A strong will, a resolute will, is needed; a will which is not to be broken by difficulties or turned aside by trifling obstacles; a determination to be a saint and not to faint and falter because the way seems long and hard and narrow. A big heart, a courageous heart, is needed for sanctification, to fight our worst enemy - our own self-love."

School days ended and he chose his path in life, sensing that the diocesan priesthood was what God was calling him to. His brother, Charlie, had already decided to become a priest entering Religious Life with the Society of Jesus, more commonly known as the Jesuits. Unexpectedly, after a series of visits to his brother's novitiate, Willie too felt that this was where God was calling him. Consequently, in March 1891, his soon to be novice master met a young, high-spirited boy skipping his way up the steps to the door of the novitiate. The older man noted this joy as a sign of a genuine vocation - of course, this premonition was to prove right.

The Novice

Willie would spend the next fifteen years in religious formation, preparing for his hoped for ordination as a Jesuit priest. It was not to be without its sufferings. During this time he was plagued with ill health, to such an extent that it almost prevented him continuing in his studies. Nevertheless, he persevered, seeing it all as part of God's plan for him. At school, he had been observed as headstrong and impetuous - good qualities, albeit in need of disciplining. As a young man he set about the hard task of training these qualities to serve God. His other traits of temperament so far displayed - a devout faith, a love of all regardless of station in life, a willingness to throw himself into what he felt was right (in other words piety, charity, a firm resolve) - all these began to coalesce and mature. They were to be supplemented further by a spiritual training that had but one aim: to make him a saint. During these important years, that particular aim increasingly crystallised to such an extent that it would be fair to say that sanctity became his life's great quest:

> "I feel within me a constant desire or craving for holiness, a longing for prayer and a great attraction for mortification. Even walking along the streets I

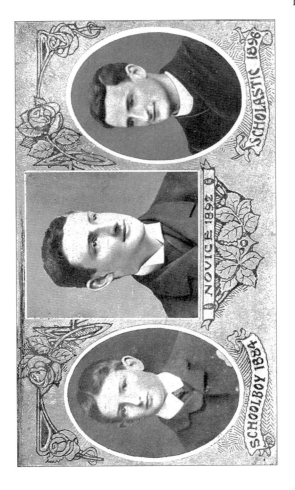

SCHOLASTIC 1896

NOVICE 1892

SCHOOLBOY 1884

feel God tugging at my heart and, in a sweet loving way, urging, urging, urging me to give myself up absolutely to Him and His service. Over and over again I say, 'My God, I will become a saint since You ask it.' But there is no progress, no real effort. The truth is, I am afraid of the sacrifice, afraid of doing what God wants; and I delude myself into thinking I am doing God's will and satisfying Him by an empty promise. What an abuse of grace! This cannot go on. I feel there must be a change now... an absolute surrender to all God wants."

The Jesuit

Those same characteristics that had marked him out at school were once more evident as a religious. His smiling, attractive demeanour combined with high spirits and pranks was still evident for all to see. What most did not see beneath this external façade was an ever-deepening love of God, and a dawning sense of the uncompromising nature of such love. For he had begun to realise that what was being asked of him was nothing less than 'everything'. All had to be surrendered to God alone. Like all mystics, the thrill of what was occurring - all interior - was worthy of the greatest romances as it surpassed and transcended any earthly affection. This was the passionate nature of the young Willie Doyle.

As part of his formation, he was assigned to Clongowes Wood College, a Jesuit school in County Kildare. In what could have been a prosaic existence, he responded by seeing it all as the will of God and set about winning souls precisely where God had placed him. And so, by example alone, he proceeded to win the hearts, then the souls, of the boys around him. In fact, as was later noted, it would be fair to say that the whole school fell under his spell. Often a charismatic personality can effect much more through a 'presence' than by anything that is said; such was the case with the new young master, Willie Doyle. And this presence, earlier noted at school, had begun to be purified. It was something others perceived as holiness. Reading accounts of his life, it becomes clear that very few who came into his orbit were not touched by his presence, even if on a merely human level. And for some, a simple word or even a smile was enough to change the course of their lives.

The Priest

Willie Doyle was ordained a priest at Milltown Park, Dublin, on 28th July 1907. Immediately afterwards, he undertook the Long Retreat. As was the custom for all newly ordained Jesuits, for just under a month, the young priest would pray and reflect alone in the silence of God. It was to prove a formative experience. He began his diary account of it thus:

"I feel a great desire and determination to make this retreat as I have never made one before, for I know this is the turning point in my life - I can never be the same again.

"If I am faithful to the resolution of 'doing all things perfectly', I shall effectually cut away the numerous faults in all my actions… I shall have a fierce battle to fight with the devil and myself. But I begin with great hope and confidence, for since Jesus has inspired me to make these resolutions and urged me on till I did so, His grace will not be wanting to aid me at every step.

"In the name of God, then, I enter upon the Narrow Path which leads to sanctity, walking bravely on in imitation of my Jesus Who is by my side carrying His

> Cross. To imitate Him and make my life resemble
> His in some small degree, will be my life's work, that
> so I may be worthy to die for Him."

Thereafter, now finally ordained, he went forth an apostle
with all the force that had been building up in his interior life.
Initially, assigned to the Jesuit Mission Staff, his apostolate
was to give missions and retreats wherever he was sent. Over
the coming years, Father Willie would give hundreds. His
first two are noteworthy, however. Within days of his arrival
in Aberdeen, fellow veteran missioners were more than
satisfied with how easily their 'novice' had taken to his task.
As was to be expected, with his natural gifts, demeanour and
eloquence, Father Doyle excelled at preaching. This was
coupled with a deep spiritual power, born of a life of prayer
and penance, that invariably drew souls to closer to Christ,
especially in and through the Sacrament of Confession.

> "I have not met a single refusal to come to the mission
> or to confession so far during my missionary career.
> Why should there be one because Jesus for some
> mysterious reason seems to delight in using perhaps
> the most wretched of all His priests as the channel of
> His grace? When I go to see a hard hopeless case, I
> cannot describe what happens exactly, but I seem to
> be able to lift up my heart like a cup and pour grace
> and the love of God upon that poor soul. I can see
> the result instantly, almost like the melting of snow."

Great Yarmouth was his next port of call. Here again hearts were moved; souls cleansed; lives transformed. And hardened sinners returned while the weak were made stronger and the strong strove for sanctity - none remained unmoved. Through this demanding work, an ever-increasing joy grew, as well as a deeper understanding of his call. During these next years, his life would be a seemingly endless series of retreats and missions; weeks of preaching combined with long hours in the confessional, before even longer nights of prayer and penances in reparation for sin. What had been asked was total and, from now on, he intended that nothing would be held back.

"My success here has far surpassed anything I looked for. But it is, of course, the work of God's grace. I do not think I could possibly find food for vainglory in anything I have done no more than an organ grinder prides himself on the beautiful music he produces by turning a handle. God knows I only wish and seek His greater glory, and to make others love Him, if I cannot love Him myself? All along I felt it was all His doing, and that I was just a mere instrument in His hands, and a wretched one at that. All through I had the feeling that I was like an old bucket full of holes, which broke the poor Lord's Heart as He tried to carry His precious grace into the hearts of His children."

It is not surprising, no doubt an echo of his past concern for the poor, to find him later at the forefront of a drive to bring so-called Workers' Retreats to Ireland. Started on the Continent, and after some success in the Low Countries, the idea spread to England through his fellow Jesuit, Father Plater, who, in turn, encouraged his Irish confrère to bring this much-needed apostolate to his native land. As it happened, Father Doyle had already begun to pioneer such initiatives. Nevertheless, he was hesitant about the long-term success of such a venture. Such thoughts were soon pushed aside, however, on receiving a delegation of workers from the Guinness Brewery in Dublin. These men made it clear that not only did they want to participate in the proposed retreats but, through the sweat of their labour, they wanted to help turn this, as yet theoretical idea, into concrete reality. Thereafter, work began on part of the recently purchased Rathfarnam Castle, and soon it was converted into the Dublin Diocese's Centre for Workers' Retreats. This work had now found a home.

"This morning during Mass I felt strongly that Jesus was pained that you do not trust Him absolutely, that is trust Him in every detail of your life. You are wanting in that childlike confidence He desires so much from you, the taking lovingly and trustfully from His hands all that He sends you, not even wishing things to have happened otherwise. He wants you to possess your soul in peace in the midst of the many troubles, cares and difficulties of your work, looking upon everything as arranged by Him, and hence something to welcome joyfully. Jesus will not dwell in your soul as He wishes unless you are at peace. This is the first step towards that union which you desire so much - but not so much as He does. Don't keep Him waiting, my child, but by earnest and constant efforts empty your heart of every care that He may abide with you for ever."

From the start, Father Doyle had been noted for his eloquence in the pulpit. Soon he was to demonstrate this in another art form: as a pamphleteer.

The pamphlets he wrote were to be huge sellers throughout the English-speaking world, and influenced a whole generation in discerning a vocation. *Shall I be a Priest* (1915) and *Vocations* (1913) became more successful than their author could ever have imagined possible. It was not the power of the well-judged word alone that shone through his writing, however. It was the author's own authentic vocation. It was this that pointed the reader towards what really mattered, namely, the peace and joy that comes from doing the will of God. As it transpired, he managed to communicate this on the written page as easily as he had in the pulpit, the confessional, the convent parlour or the classroom. As a result, vocations came thick and fast. Many would later tell of how they owed the beginnings of their life-long offering to the author of these pamphlets.

"My little book on Vocations has brought me a good deal of consolation lately. The Superior of X told me they had at least two novices whose thoughts had been first directed to religious life by reading the pamphlet and that another, whose vocation was due in great measure to the book, was expected in a few days from Australia. Yesterday I had a letter from the Fathers in London telling me several of their young men had been led to take the final step by the same means. Some time ago a Lutheran, recently received into the Church, wrote from New York saying that the pamphlet had appealed to him so much that he was now studying for the priesthood. This is encouraging and proves what I have always held, that there are vocations in abundance if only they were helped a little."

The Hunter of Souls

A hunter of souls: Father Doyle was fearless in tracking down his prey. He was single minded in saving even the most hardened sinners from hell. Countless hours spent in the confessional were rewarded with many a 'big fish'. It appears from accounts, both his and others, that no opportunity was missed - for example, the prostitute that remembered his look and quiet words to "go home at this late hour", enough for a later conversion; or the sinner who threatened to stab the young Jesuit through the heart if he persisted. By way of reply, the priest simply opened his cassock to make it all the easier for the knife to plunge into his heart. Stunned, the man thought better of it, and soon after confessed all. Seemingly he was beaten by the priest's good-humoured humanity; however, this belied the deadly earnestness with which Father Willie pursued this 'greatest game of all'. In the end, it seems that sinners, both 'big' and 'small', never stood a chance, arraigned as they were, against the priest's hours of prayer and mortification.

Nevertheless, Father Willie was well aware that in this fight for souls there was no time to waste and moreover, that only united with Christ could such a fight be propagated at all. As a result, and for this purpose, his life was dedicated to the ever-closer union with his Saviour.

"My intense desire and longing is to make others love Jesus and to draw them to His Sacred Heart. Recently at Mass I have found myself at the Dominus Vobiscum opening my arms wide with the intention of embracing every soul present and drawing them in spite of themselves into that Heart which longs for their love. 'Compel them to come in,' Jesus said. Yes, compel them to dive into that abyss of love. Sometimes, I might say nearly always, when speaking to people I am seized with an extraordinary desire to draw their hearts to God. I could go down on my knees before them and beg them to be pure and holy, so strong do I feel the longing of Jesus for sanctity in everyone, and since I may not do this, I try to do what I find hard to describe in words - to pour out of my heart any grace or love of God there may be in it, and then with all the force of my will to draw their hearts into that of Jesus."

The Penitent

"To-day while praying in the Chapel, suddenly it seemed to me as if I were standing before a narrow path all choked with briars and sharp thorns. Jesus was beside me with a large cross and I heard Him ask me would I strip myself of all things, and naked as He was on Calvary, take that cross on my bare shoulders and bravely fight my way to the end of the road. I realised clearly that this would mean much suffering and that very soon my flesh would be torn and bleeding from the thorns. All the same, humbly I promised Him, that, relying on His grace, I would not shrink from what He asked, and even begged Him to drag me through these briars since I am so cowardly. This inspiration, coming so soon after the ardent desire really to crucify myself, shows me clearly what kind of life Jesus is asking from me. I felt impelled to resolve as far as possible never to be without some slight bodily suffering, e.g. chain on arm, etc. I have also made a vow twice (binding for one day) to refuse on that day no sacrifice which I really feel my Jesus asks from me. All this has given me great interior peace and happiness, with fresh courage and determination to become a saint. Life is too short for a truce."

Inevitably, Father Willie's identification with Christ led him ever closer to the figure of the Crucified Saviour. Daily, he sought to incarnate this reality into his own life - not least through the age-old practices of Christian asceticism. At meal times, he denied himself not only the superfluous but also the necessary. The constant guarding of his senses, not least his eyes, was perpetual. So too was the 'dry' mortification of accounting for every minute of each day. This spiritual recording would become as endless as it proved rewarding: a spiritual practice he would regularly recommend to others. In addition, as was customary amongst some religious, he resorted to the penitential use of the discipline. All of this was combined with long hours of prayer. Many nights would be punctuated with nocturnal watches. On one occasion, and solely motivated by love, he rose in the dead of night and went to the darkness of a damp cellar to kneel for hours upon its cold stones. There were other penances he noted. At Rathfarnam Castle on a winter's night, he would immerse himself in the ice-cold waters of its lake. At night too, he would walk barefoot in pilgrimage to a nearby shrine. These were all done in reparation for sins, both his and others, but especially for those of priests. This was a dramatic and unusual path, but one that seems to have been taken with the complete cognizance and agreement of his then spiritual director. Early in the path he had been given, Father Willie realised that it would be a never-ending battle against self, with no quarter given. Now, at last, it appeared that the boy who had stood in front of the mirror at Lent had finally come of age.

It must be stated that to some of his contemporaries, who learned of these practices only after his death, this all seemed strange, macabre even. That verdict, perhaps all too understandable, appears to judge the times not the man. Especially given that such a judgement overlooked the horrors of the then recent war, with its endlessly cruel suffering orchestrated for no other reason than nationalism, and that in the end claimed the life of this penitent soul. No, there was nothing here other than a man, like his Master before him, making lamentation with the prayer of the body. Its only rationale was repentance, both his own and that of others. And through it all, his eyes were firmly fixed upon nothing less than the greatest act of love itself: Calvary. Without understanding that, all mortifications would indeed appear 'meaningless'; however, for Father Willie they were anything but that. Engaged in the 'eternal battle', alone in that damp cellar, he was offering all for sinners. This was no gloomy ascetic, but, rather, a spiritual warrior in the full heat of combat with the perennial enemies: the Devil, the World and Self.

"Heroism is a virtue which has an attraction for every heart. It seems to lift us out of our petty selves and make us for a moment forget our own selfish interests. It appeals irresistibly to the noble-minded; to the cowardly even, it is a powerful stimulus. Thus it is that in all times the saints have ever had such an attraction for men - they are heroes! In their secret hidden lives of prayer and penance, men saw a heroism which was not the one sharp pang of a fearless deed, leaving their names to history as a nation's pride, but a nobler heroism of a life of countless noble deeds, unknown perhaps to man; by God alone were their secret victories seen."

The Military Chaplain

"I want you to know what I went through by volunteering for the Front. God made me feel with absolute certainty - I suppose to increase the merit of the offering - that I shall be killed. The struggle was hard, for I did not want to die; not indeed that I am afraid of death, but the thought that I could never again do more for God or suffer for Him in heaven made the sacrifice too bitter for words."

A year later after these words were written, in November 1915, his wish was granted. By then, he was with the 8th Battalion of the Royal Irish Fusiliers at Borden Camp, Hampshire, prior to departure for France. Already, he had quickly and easily fitted into military life. No doubt, the environment reminded him of school, to say nothing of his later years as a religious; hierarchical structure with its clear sense of order would have been second nature to a Jesuit. Nevertheless, Father Doyle never forgot that he was there first and foremost as a priest - his 'flock' was now the officers and soldiers of his battalion. For them, he was prepared to spare nothing, down to the last drop of his blood if necessary. And all with one aim, the only thing he considered worth dying for: their salvation.

Father Willie was to find the theatre of war a fertile soil. He discovered war was no time for petty concerns but that it concentrated the mind on larger questions - life, death, heaven and hell. And so, from now on, his 'flock' was to prove as demanding, as he was to prove unrelenting.

"...What decided me in the end was a thought that flashed into my mind when in the chapel: the thought that if I get killed I shall die a martyr of charity and so the longing of my heart will be gratified. This much my offering myself as chaplain has done for me: it has made me realise that my life may be very short and that I must do all I can for Jesus now.

"I long to go and shed my blood for Jesus and, if He wills it, to die a martyr of charity. The thought that at any moment I may be called to the Front, perhaps to die, has roused a great desire to do all I can while I have life. I feel great strength to make any sacrifice and little difficulty in doing so. I may not have long now to prove my love for Jesus."

Father Willie Doyle, Military Chaplain, 1915.

The Front

From the moment of landing in France, the lot of the Tommy was misery. In this regard, the fate of the Royal Irish Fusiliers was to be no different. On their disembarkation on the Continent, they became part of the then prevailing military stalemate. For years, the two heavily armed combatants had been interminably blasting each other at close range in an attempt to break the deadlock - all of which had proved futile. Thousands had died; many others were about to do so, whilst even more were to lose their lives through disease, to say nothing of the wounded, maimed and disfigured.

From now on, the daily lot of the new padre was to be unrelenting: poor food and little rest, unhygienic and often flooded trenches, plus the never-ending noise of warfare. Nevertheless, through it all, he was determined to share every moment with his comrades. Tellingly, from the start, he eschewed the officer's horse, instead opting to march each and every mile with the ranks, regardless of weather or fatigue. Where they went, so did he; sharing in every new horror along the way. How could any of them forget the night the battalion marched through - and over - a field fresh with corpses? At this point, even his vivid turn of phrase, a noted characteristic in his letters home, falls silent at such an experience.

There was to be little rest at the Front. What sleep there was took place in a muddy dug-out that barely held Father Doyle's long body. He would often awake, body soaked through with, on occasion, a rat sitting on his face. This was a daily occurrence, coupled with the threat of attack that was as constant as it was real. When not wholly unexpectedly, his dug-out was finally destroyed after having taken a direct hit from a German shell, his reaction was to joke that he was nostalgic for its former pleasures. Needless to say, whatever else had occurred, at least outwardly, his humour did not desert him. Instead, all noted his constant smile and good cheer. In the misery of daily life at the Front this did not go unnoticed by the men he served.

As time progressed, he became used to putting a 'brave face' on such sufferings and privations. Only in some of his letters home would he reveal the true cost of war and all its horrors. And yet, in the midst of it all, the mystic within him was awakened to the fact that, even here, in the mud and blood, Christ was drawing him ever closer. Such an experience occurred during an uncharacteristic cessation in the fighting at Loos. During this lull, Father Willie Doyle wandered out alone into the then silent field of battle. There he found an unusual, if comforting, monument to the source of both his mission and inner peace.

"I had an opportunity, a rare one, thanks to the fog, of examining closely in daylight one of the wonders of the war, the famous Crucifix or Calvary of Loos. This is a very large cross standing on a mound in a most exposed position, the centre of fierce fighting. One of the four trees standing by it has been torn up by a shell, the branches of the others smashed to bits, a tombstone at its feet lies broken in half and the houses on either side are a heap of ruins. But neither cross nor figure has been touched. I looked closely and could not see even one bullet hole. Surely if the Almighty can protect the image of His Son, it will be no great difficulty to guard His priest also, as indeed He has done in a wonderful way."

The padre had marched to the battlefront with his battalion. This battalion, 'his men', was Irish and predominately Catholic. It comes as no surprise to learn that his presence amongst them had a deep resonance - something he was to comment upon on a number of occasions. The soldiers for their part valued him as a 'man of God', not least as the means by which to help 'settle their account' with the Almighty before 'closing time'. But that was not the whole story. For they sensed, like the schoolboys and mission-goers before them, that here was a true man of faith. Although it was not something they would have been able to articulate, they were witnessing someone who had become in effect: *alter Christus* - 'another Christ'. And so, they watched as in their midst, the priest tended them like the true Shepherd of the Flock. Knowing the lengths he would go to ensure that, when that final moment came, one anticipated with such terror, and when all they had ever known was passing before their eyes, he would be there: to anoint, absolve, with Viaticum... And they were proved right. For even when lying helpless, cut adrift in the dreaded 'No Man's Land,' they knew Father Willie would find them, often dodging enemy machine guns to do so. They were his 'flock', and he was no hireling.

"I don't think you will blame me when I tell you that more than once the words of Absolution stuck in my throat, and the tears splashed down on the patient suffering faces of my poor boys as I leant down to anoint them. One young soldier seized my two hands and covered them with kisses; another looked up and said: 'Oh! Father I can die happy now, sure I'm not afraid of death or anything else since I have seen you.' Don't you think, dear father, that the little sacrifice made in coming out here has already been more than repaid, and if you have suffered a little anxiety on my account, you have at least the consolation of knowing that I have, through God's goodness, been able to comfort many a poor fellow and perhaps to open the gates of Heaven for them."

In the months that followed, one struggles to imagine the horrors he experienced on a daily basis: days that included anointing soldiers so badly wounded that they no longer had faces; or endlessly holding in his arms the dying. Some of these were barely more than boys gasping their final prayer before that familiar serene smile would pass over a now impassive face. And then there was the sorry task of burying what was left of them, no matter what the dangers. Giving the dead a Christian burial was an obligation that Father Willie Doyle took seriously, often doing so with his bare hands.

"The cemetery, part of a field, was outside the town in the open country, so exposed to shell and rifle fire that it could not be approached by day.

"As soon as it was dark we carried the poor fellow out on a stretcher, just as he had fallen, and as quietly as we could began to dig the grave. It was weird. We were standing in front of the German trenches on two sides, though a fair distance away, and every now and then a star-shell went up which we felt certain would reveal our presence to the enemy. I put my ritual in the bottom of my hat and with the aid of an electric torch read the burial service, while the men screened the light with their caps, for a single flash would have turned the machine guns on us. I cannot say if we were seen or not, but all the time bullets came whizzing by, though more than likely stray ones and not aimed at us. Once I had to get the men to lie down as things were rather warm; but somehow felt quite safe, as if the dead soldier's guardian angel was sheltering us from all danger, till the poor dust was laid to rest. It was my first war burial though assuredly not my last. May God rest his soul and comfort those left to mourn him."

His letters from the Front, often to his father, are revealing. In the midst of what he described as "hell", what can be gleaned from them, nevertheless, was his priestly soul, longing for the Reign of Christ the King in all hearts throughout the world. With the eyes of the mystic, he went further still, seeing war itself as an occasion when those around him, at last, had begun to realise the true meaning of life, for some just in time. In the daily carnage, however, time was running out for many; it would be the last time that their soul could be saved for Christ. This was the source of the urgency that drove him on again and again in those never-ending forays into that desperate uncertainty called 'No Man's Land'.

"Taking a short cut across country to our lines I found myself on the first battle field of Loos, the place where the French had made their attack. For some reason or other this part of the ground has not been cleared, and it remains more or less as it was the morning after the fight. I had to pick my steps, for numbers of unexploded shells, bombs and grenades lay all round. The ground was littered with broken rifles, torn uniforms, packs, etc., just as the men had flung them aside, charging the German trenches. Almost the first thing I saw was a human head torn from the trunk, though there was no sign of the body. The soldiers had been buried on the spot they fell; that is, if you can call burial, hastily throwing a few shovelfuls of clay on the corpses: there was little time, I fancy, for digging graves, and in war time there is not much thought or sentiment for the slain. As I walked along, I wondered had they made certain each man was really dead. One poor fellow had been buried, surely, before the breath had left his body, for there was every sign of a last struggle and one arm was thrust out from its shroud of clay. A large mound caught my eye. Four pairs of feet were sticking out, one a German, judging by his boots, and three Frenchmen - friend and foe are sleeping their long last sleep in peace together. They were decently covered compared with the next I saw; a handful of earth covered the wasted body, but the legs and arms and head were exposed to view. He seemed quite a young lad, with fair, almost golden, hair. 'An unknown soldier' was all the rough wooden cross over him told me about him; but I thought of the sorrowing mother, far away, thinking of her boy who was 'missing' and hoping against hope that he might one day come back. Thank God, Heaven one day will reunite them both. I found a shovel near at hand, and after a couple of hours' stiff work was able to cover the bodies decently, so that on earth at least they might rest in peace."

Near miss after near miss from the deadly German shells, made little difference to the priest in his mission. Constantly running a gauntlet of gunfire, he proved fearless. Soon, by way of official recognition, Father Willie Doyle was awarded the Military Cross. By all accounts, however, it should have been the Victoria Cross, the highest decoration for bravery, but politics played their part, and he was passed over. It was later said he had three hindrances: being Irish, Catholic and a Jesuit. In any event, the award meant nothing to him. His battle plan was not that of his fellow officers - his had always involved a different sort of battle, one that commenced on the day of his ordination. The circumstances of the 'warfare' may have changed, from school and church to stagnant trench and blasted battlefield, but it had made little difference - he was to be busy about his General's work.

Father Willie celebrated his first Holy Mass in the trenches on 23rd April 1916, Easter Sunday:

"My church was a bit of a trench, the altar a pile of sandbags. Though we had to stand deep in mud, not knowing the moment a sudden call to arms would come, many a fervent prayer went up to heaven that morning.

"I had never celebrated Mass in the open before, and I think the men were as much impressed as I was. It was a glorious morning with just a sufficient spice of danger to give the necessary warlike touch to the picture by the presence of a German aeroplane scouting near at hand. I was a wee bit anxious lest a bomb might come down in the middle of the men, but I fancy our unwelcome visitor had quite enough to do, dodging the shells from our guns which kept booming all during Mass; besides I felt confident that for once our guardian angels would do their duty and protect us all till Mass was over. When I finished breakfast, I found a big number of men waiting for Confession. I gave them Communion as well, though they were not fasting, as they were going to the trenches that evening and being in danger of death could receive the Blessed Sacrament as Viaticum. It was the last Communion for many poor fellows who, I trust, are praying for me in Heaven now.

"All day I have been busy hearing the men's confessions, and giving batch after batch Holy

Communion. A consolation surely to see them crowding to the Sacraments, but a sad one too, because I know for many of them it is the last Absolution they will ever receive, and the next time they meet our Blessed Lord will be when they see Him face to face in Heaven."

In the midst of this deadly chaos, only prayer could sustain him. Alone in the trenches, Father Willie still found time to adore the Eucharistic Presence, with the very Prince of Peace hung around his neck in a Pyx, whilst all around him the only sounds to accompany these acts of adoration were those of hell.

"Jesus has long urged me to give Him a whole night of prayer and reparation. Last night I prayed in my dug-out at Kemmel from 9 till 5 (eight hours), most of the time on my knees. I bound myself beforehand to do so by vow in order not to let myself off. Though I had only two hours' sleep, I am not very tired or weary today. Jesus wants more of these nights of prayer, adoration and atonement."

The Gas Attack

One particular letter home needs little by way of annotation. It describes what was feared most in the trenches, not the shelling or gunfire, but an even deadlier and more far-reaching enemy: gas. As we read, however, the priest, as ever, had but one concern.

"I saw both right and left of where I stood the green wave of a second gas attack rolling towards me like some huge spectre stretching out its ghostly arms. As I saw it coming, my heart went out to God in one fervent act of gratitude for His goodness to me. As probably you know we all carry 'smoke helmets' slung over our shoulders in a case, to be used against a gas attack. That morning as I was leaving my dugout I threw my helmet aside. I had a fairly long walk before me, the helmet is a bit heavy on a hot day, and as I said, German gas was most unlikely. So I made up my mind to leave it behind. In view of what happened, it may appear imagination now, but a voice seemed to whisper loudly in my ear: 'Take your helmet with you; don't leave without it'. I turned back and slung it over my shoulder. Surely it was the warning voice of my guardian angel, for if I had not done so, you would never have had this letter.

"I wonder can you picture my feelings at this moment? Here was death in its most awful form sweeping down towards me…it was an anxious moment waiting for the scorching test, and to make things more horrible, I was absolutely alone. But I had the companionship of One Who sustained me in the hour of trial, and kneeling down I took the Pyx from my pocket and received the Blessed Eucharist as Viaticum. I had not a moment to spare, and had my helmet just fixed when I was buried in a thick green fog of poison gas. In a few moments my confidence returned for the helmet worked perfectly and I found I was able to breathe without any ill effects from the gas.

"By the time I got down to the dressing station the guns had ceased fire, the gas blown away, and the sun was shining in a cloudless sky. Already a stream of wounded was coming in and I soon had my hands full, when an urgent message reached me from the front trench. A poor fellow had been desperately wounded, a bullet had cut him like a knife across the stomach, with results you can best imagine. He was told he had only a few minutes to live, and asked if they could do anything for him. 'I have only one wish before I die' he answered, 'could you possibly get me Fr Doyle? I'll go happy then.' It was hard work to reach him, as parts of the communication trench were knee deep in water and thick mud. Then I was misdirected and sent in the wrong direction, but I kept on praying I might be in time, and at last found the dying man still breathing and conscious. The look of joy, which lit up his face when I knelt beside him, was reward enough for the effort I had made. I gave him Absolution and anointed him before he died, but occupied as I was I did not notice that a third gas attack had begun. Before I could get my helmet out and on, I had swallowed a couple of mouthfuls, which did me no serious harm beyond making me feel rather sick and weak.

"As I made my way slowly up the trench, feeling altogether 'a poor thing,' I stumbled across a young officer who had been badly gassed. He had got his helmet on, but was coughing and choking in a terrible way. 'For God's sake,' he cried, 'help me to tear off this helmet - I can't breathe. I'm dying.' I saw if I left him the end would not be far; so catching hold of him, I half carried, half dragged him up the trench to the medical aid post. I shall never forget that ten minutes, it seemed hours. I seemed to have lost all my strength: struggling with him to prevent him killing himself by tearing off his helmet made me forget almost how to breathe through mine. I was almost stifled, though safe from gas, while the perspiration simply poured from my forehead. I could do nothing but pray for help and set my teeth, for if I once let go, he was a dead man. Thank God, we both at last got to the aid post…I was lying on the stretcher going to 'peg out,' as the doctor believed, God gave me back my strength and energy in a way which was nothing short of a miracle, to help many a poor fellow to die in peace and perhaps to open the gates of heaven to not a few.

"I had come through the three attacks without ill results, though having been unexpectedly caught by the last one, as I was anointing a dying man and did not see the poisonous fumes coming, I had swallowed some of the gas before I could get my helmet on… There was little time to think of that, for wounded and dying were lying all along the trenches, and I was the only priest on that section at the time. …It was impossible to do one's work with the gas helmet on, and so as I knelt down to absolve or anoint man after man for the greater part of that day, I had to inhale the chlorine fumes…In happy ignorance of my real state, I covered mile after mile of those trenches until at last in the evening, when the work was done, I was able to rejoin my battalion in a village close to the Line.

"I fell asleep only to be rudely awakened at four next morning by the crash of guns and the dreaded bugle call 'gas alarm, gas alarm.' The Germans had launched a second attack, fiercer than the first. It did not take long to make up my mind what to do - who would hesitate at such a moment, when the Reaper Death was busy? - and before I reached the trenches I had anointed a number of poor fellows who had struggled back after being gassed and had fallen dying by the roadside.

"But now it is evident many of the men despised the 'old German gas,' some did not bother putting on their helmets, others had torn theirs, and others like myself had thrown them aside or lost them. From early morning till late at night I worked my way from trench to trench single handed the first day, with three regiments to look after, and could get no help. Many men died before I could reach them; others seemed just to live till I anointed them, and were gone before I passed back. There they lay, scores of them (we lost 800, nearly all from gas) in the bottom of the trench, in every conceivable posture of human agony: the clothes torn off their bodies in a vain effort to breathe; while from end to end of that valley of death came one low unceasing moan from the lips of brave men fighting and struggling for life."

The Somme

As if this was not horror enough, Father Willie Doyle was soon after to march with his battalion to a place synonymous with the worst of the industrial slaughter that was the Great War - later simply known as: The Somme.

"I was standing about 100 yards away watching a party of my men crossing the valley, when I saw the earth under their feet open and the twenty men disappear in a cloud of smoke, while a column of stones and clay was shot a couple of hundred feet into the air. A big German shell by the merest chance had landed in the middle of the party. I rushed down the slope, getting a most unmerciful 'whack' between the shoulders, probably from a falling stone, as it did not wound me, but it was no time to think of one's safety. I gave them all a General Absolution, scraped the clay from the faces of a couple of buried men who were not wounded, and then anointed as many of the poor lads as I could reach. Two of them had no faces to anoint and others were ten feet under the clay, but a few were living still. By this time half a dozen volunteers had run up and were digging the buried men out. War may be horrible, but it certainly brings out the best side of a man's character;

over and over again I have seen men risking their lives to help or save a comrade, and these brave fellows knew the risk they were taking, for when a German shell falls in a certain place, you clear as quickly as you can since several more are pretty certain to land close. It was a case of duty for me, but real courage for them. We dug like demons for our lads' lives and our own, to tell the truth, for every few minutes another 'iron pill' from a Krupp gun would come tearing down the valley, making our very hearts leap into our mouths. More than once we were well sprinkled with clay and stones, but the cup of cold water promise was well kept, and not one of the party received a scratch. We got three buried men out alive, not much the worse for their trying experience, but so thoroughly had the shell done its work that there was not a single wounded man in the rest of the party; all had gone to a better land. As I walked back I nearly shared the fate of my boys, but somehow escaped again, and pulled out two more lads who were only buried up to the waist and uninjured. Meanwhile the regiment had been ordered back to a safer position on the hill, and we were able to breathe once more.

"The first part of our journey lay through a narrow trench, the floor of which consisted of deep thick mud, and the bodies of dead men trodden under foot. It was horrible beyond description, but there was no help for it, and on the half-rotten corpses of our own brave men we marched in silence, everyone busy with his own thoughts. I shall spare you gruesome details, but you can picture one's sensations as one felt the ground yield under one's foot, and one sank down through the body of some poor fellow.

"Half an hour of this brought us out on the open into the middle of the battlefield of some days previous. The wounded, at least I hope so, had all been removed, but the dead lay there stiff and stark, with open staring eyes, just as they had fallen. Good God, such a sight! I had tried to prepare myself for this, but all I had read or pictured gave me little idea of the reality. Some lay as if they were sleeping quietly, others had died in agony, or had had the life crushed out of them by mortal fear, while the whole ground, every foot of it, was littered with heads or limbs or pieces of torn human bodies. In the bottom of one hole lay a British and a German soldier, locked in a deadly embrace, neither had any weapon, but they had fought on to the bitter end. Another couple seemed to have realised that the horrible struggle was none of their making, and that they were both children of the same God; they had died hand-in-hand praying for and forgiving one another. A third face caught my eye, a tall, strikingly handsome young German, not more, I should say, than eighteen. He lay there calm and peaceful, with a smile of happiness on his face, as if he had had a glimpse of Heaven before he died. Ah, if only his poor mother could have seen her boy it would have soothed the pain of her broken heart.

"I have been through the most terrible experience of my whole life, in comparison with which all that I have witnessed or suffered since my arrival in France seems of little consequence; a time of such awful horror that I believe if the good God had not helped me powerfully by His grace I could never have endured it. To sum up all in one word, for the past week I have been living literally in hell, amid sights and scenes and dangers enough to test the courage of the bravest; but through it all my confidence and trust in our Blessed Lord's protection never wavered, for I felt that somehow, even if it needed a miracle, He would bring me safe through the furnace of tribulation. I was hit three times, on the last occasion by a piece of shell big enough to have taken off half my leg, but wonderful to relate I did, as you can imagine, not receive a wound or scratch...I am pretty well worn out and exhausted, rather shaken by the terrific strain of those days and nights without any real sleep or repose, with nerves tingling…but it is all over now..."

The tenth anniversary of his ordination was spent at the Front. Where he was, however, by then made little difference. Father Doyle had, in effect, become a 'living monstrance' - carrying the Bread of Life to the dying in a battlefield now seemingly as dark as the Valley of Death itself.

"I have been living in the front trenches for the last week, in a sea of mud, drenched to the skin with rain and mercilessly peppered with all sorts and conditions of shells. Yet I realize that some strange purifying process is going on in my soul, and that this life is doing much for my sanctification. This much I can say: I hunger and thirst for holiness, and for humiliations and sufferings, which are the short-cut to holiness; though when these things do come, I often pull a long face and try to avoid them. Yet lately I have come to understand as never before that it is only 'through many tribulations' we can hope to enter the Promised Land of sanctity. I think when this war is over (about twenty years hence) I shall become a hermit! I never felt so utterly sick of the world and worldlings. All this bustle and movement has wearied my soul beyond measure. I am longing for solitude, to be alone with Jesus, for He seems to fill every want in my life. All the same as the days go by I thank our Blessed Lord more and more for the grace of getting out here. Not exactly because of the consolation of helping so many poor fellows or because of the merit the hard life must bring with it, but because I feel this experience has influenced my whole future, which I cannot further explain except by saying that God has given me the grace of my life since I came.

"Then in addition there is the great privilege and joy of carrying our dear Lord next to my heart day and night.

…Little did I think then that the God of holiness would stoop so low as to make me His resting-place. Why this favour alone would be worth going through twenty wars for! I feel ashamed at times that I do not profit more by His nearness, but I know that He makes allowances for weak inconstant nature, and that even when I do not directly think of Him, He is silently working in my soul. Do you not think that Jesus must have done very much for Mary during the nine months she bore Him within her? I feel that He will do much, very much, for me too whilst I carry Him about with me.

"Sometimes God seems to leave me to my weakness and I tremble with fear. At other times I have so much trust and confidence in His loving protection that I could almost sit down on a bursting shell feeling I could come to no harm. You would laugh, or perhaps cry, if you saw me at this moment sitting on a pile of bricks and rubbish. Shells are bursting some little distance away on three sides and occasionally a piece comes down with an unpleasantly close thud. But what does it matter? Jesus is resting on my heart, and whenever I like I can fold my arms over Him and press Him to that heart which, as He knows, beats with love of Him.

"He has shielded me from almost countless dangers with more than the tender care of an earthly mother - what I have to say sounds in parts almost like a fairy tale - and if He has tried my endurance, once at least almost to breaking point, it was only to fill me with joy at the thought that I 'was deemed worthy to suffer (a little) for Him'.

"By cutting a piece out of the side of the trench, I was just able to stand in front of my tiny altar, a biscuit box supported on two German bayonets. God's angels, no doubt, were hovering overhead, but so were the shells, hundreds of them, and I was a little afraid that when the earth shook with the crash of the guns, the chalice might be overturned. Round about me on every side was the biggest congregation I ever had: behind the altar, on either side, and in front, row after row, sometimes crowding one upon the other, but all quiet and silent, as if they were straining their ears to catch every syllable of that tremendous act of Sacrifice - but every man was dead! Some had lain there for a week and were foul and horrible to look at, with faces black and green. Others had only just fallen, and seemed rather sleeping than dead, but there they lay, for none had time to bury them, brave fellows, every one, friend and foe alike, while I held in my unworthy hands the God of Battles, their Creator and their Judge, and prayed Him to give rest to their souls. Surely that Mass for the Dead, in the midst of, and surrounded by the dead, was an experience not easily to be forgotten."

The Casualty

And so, in the spring of 1917, with what was left of his battalion, Father Willie marched to fields where the promised 'final push' to victory would take place or so the Generals claimed. The planned offensive was to pass through Passchendaele.

Over the months that followed, wave after wave of prolonged British attack met with even stiffer opposition than that originally anticipated. Inevitably, casualties mounted, whilst the ground surrendered by the enemy proved negligible. Nevertheless, throughout the padre continued his work; serving as best he could the dying at the makeshift medical centres known as Regimental Aid Posts and rushing to help the wounded in 'No Man's Land'.

"A sad morning as casualties were heavy and many men came in dreadfully wounded. One man was the bravest I ever met. He was in dreadful agony, for both legs had been blown off at the knee. But never a complaint fell from his lips, even while they dressed his wounds, and he tried to make light of his injuries. 'Thank God, Father,' he said, 'I am able to stick it out to the end. Is it not all for little Belgium?' The Extreme Unction, as I have noticed time and again, eased his bodily pain. 'I am much better now and easier, God bless you,' he said, as I left him to attend a dying man. He opened his eyes as I knelt beside him: 'Ah! Fr Doyle, Fr Doyle,' he whispered faintly, and then motioned me to bend lower as if he had some message to give. As I did so, he put his two arms round my neck and kissed me. It was all the poor fellow could do to show his gratitude that he had not been left to die alone and that he would have the consolation of receiving the Last Sacraments before he went to God. Sitting a little way off I saw a hideous bleeding object, a man with his face smashed by a shell, with one if not both eyes torn out. He raised his head as I spoke. 'Is that the priest? Thank God, I am all right now.' I took his blood-covered hands in mine as I searched his face for some whole spot on which to anoint him. I think I know better now why Pilate said 'Behold the Man' when he showed our Lord to the people".

Later on that same day, Father Willie was active once more.

"In the afternoon, while going my rounds, I was forced to take shelter in the dug-out of a young officer belonging to another regiment. For nearly two hours I was a prisoner and found out he was a Catholic from Dublin, and had been married just a month. Was this a chance visit, or did God send me

there to prepare him for death, for I had not long left
the spot when a shell burst and killed him? I carried
his body out the next day and buried him in a shell
hole, and once again I blessed that protecting Hand
which had shielded me from his fate."

The next day Father Willie offered the Holy Sacrifice for
what would be for the last time.

"Close beside us I had found the remains of a dugout
which had been blown in the previous day and three
men killed. I made up my mind to offer up Mass
there for the repose of their souls. In any case 'I did
not know a better 'ole to go to,' and to this little act
of charity I attribute the saving of my life later on
in the day. I had barely fitted up my altar when a
couple of shells burst overhead, sending the clay
tumbling down. For a moment I felt very tempted not
to continue as the place was far from safe. But later I
was glad I went on for the Holy Souls certainly came
to my aid as I did to theirs."

All around casualties continued to grow. Ceaselessly,
shells rained down on the soldiers of the 16th Irish
Division, who, by now, were locked in a titanic struggle
with German forces that could only have one victor: death.

In the midst of this fighting, a German shell was fired
randomly at British lines. As it exploded, Father Willie
was killed outright, whilst dragging a wounded man away

Remains of concrete blockhouse near Frezenberg - possibly the scene of Father Willie Doyle's death. The shed on the right is a subsequent structure.

from danger on the battlefield. Unlike the many to whom he had given a Christian burial, the priest was denied this. Instead, what was left of him was hastily interred without ceremony in a communal grave before all around was once more engulfed in the ensuing battle. In that war-ravaged field in Flanders, with his part now over, his mortal remains were laid to rest. The crash of exploding shells and the screams of the dying were his only requiem.

"The final scene of the awful tragedy is drawing to a close. Reverently the faithful few bear the dead Christ down the hill of shame, that body from which all the care of loving hands cannot remove the marks of the cruel scourge, the rending nails, the lance's gaping thrust. Into the tomb they bear Him, the burial place of a stranger, best suited to Him Who during His life had nowhere to lay His head. Reverently they lay Him down; one last, fond embrace of His own Mother before they lead her hence, and then in silence and in sorrow they leave Him, their dearest Master, to the watchful care of God's own angels. Sin has done its work! Sin has triumphed, but its very triumph will prove its own undoing."

Coda

The moment of his passing was already determined, he knew this, but, even so, for Father Willie it was unexpected - thinking, as he did, that he would outlive the conflict that had claimed so many of his comrades. Nevertheless, strangely such a death - dispatched to his 'old armchair' - could not have been more fitting: to die, as he did, amongst the officers and ranks he had so faithfully served, and whom he had indeed grown to love with a priestly soul. Throughout it all, his compassion had deepened, in spite of the barbarity he witnessed daily. Finally, on that 16th day of August 1917, the Irishman met his death as he had lived his life - in the service of others.

On that August day, however, when the German armour piercing shell exploded, it was not metal that had been pierced but hearts.

"Love of God is holiness, but the price of love is pain. Round the treasure house of His love, God has set a thorny hedge; those who would force their way through must not shrink when they feel the sharpness of the thorns piercing their very soul. But alas… how many after a step or two turn sadly back in fear, and so never reach the side of Jesus."

The news reached Ireland quickly. Shortly after, it was reported that a Fusilier, home on leave, incredulous on hearing of the priest's death, fell to his knees upon a Dublin pavement and with an anguished cry called out - "...no, not him" - before proceeding to tell an astonished crowd of onlookers of how the dead man had saved his life. At the same time, an Ulster Protestant wrote to a newspaper expressing his "feeling of loss, like no other" at the death of this Catholic padre; whilst General Hickie was heard to lament the passing of one of the best priests he had met as well as one of the bravest men. Father Willie's last letter was delivered to his father no doubt at the same time as the - dreaded - telegram telling of his son having been killed in action. With tears the old man read of his dead child's final wish: once more to visit *Melrose*, his beloved childhood home.

On 15th December 1917, General Hickie, having finally discovered the Doyle family address, wrote to the bereaved father as follows:

> "I could not say too much about your son. He was loved and reverenced by us all; his gallantry, self-sacrifice, and devotion to duty were all so well known and recognized. I think that his was the most wonderful character that I have ever known."

Battlefield of Passchendaele

When hostilities eventually ended, it was claimed that on the Western Front alone as many as 40,000 military personnel had converted to the Catholic Faith; partly, no doubt, due to the conduct of their Catholic military chaplains.

Epilogue

That is not the end, however.

For hidden in death, his remains lie waiting until a trumpet of a very different sort sounds across those now silent fields of Flanders. It is then, with his fallen comrades, and with the whole army of his spiritual ones arrayed throughout the world, that Father Willie Doyle, no doubt still wearing his mud-splattered army greatcoat, will rise to greet the triumphant, true General for whom he fought and gave his life. Only then, with the guns silenced forever, and the real Victory won at last, shall all tears finally be wiped away…

"I have long had the feeling that, since the world is growing so rapidly worse and worse and God has lost His hold, as it were, upon the hearts of men, He is looking all the more earnestly and anxiously for big things from those who are faithful to Him still. He cannot, perhaps, gather a large army round His standard, but He wants every one in it to be a Hero, absolutely and lovingly devoted to Him; if only we could get inside that magic circle of generous souls, I believe there is no grace He would not give us to help on the work He has so much at heart, our personal sanctification. Every day you live means an infallible growth in holiness which may be multiplied a thousand times by a little generosity... holiness means three things: - Love, Prayer, Sacrifice."

Appendix I

"The Orangemen will not forget a certain Roman Catholic chaplain who lies in a soldier's grave in that sinister plain beyond Ypres. He went forward and back over the battlefield with bullets whining about him, seeking out the dying and kneeling in the mud beside them to give them Absolution, walking with death with a smile on his face, watched by his men with reverence and a kind of awe until a shell burst near him and he was killed. His familiar figure was seen and welcomed by hundreds of Irishmen who lay in that bloody place. Each time he came back across the field he was begged to remain in comparative safety. Smilingly he shook his head and went again into the storm. He had been with his boys at Ginchy and through other times of stress, and he would not desert them in their agony. They remember him as a saint - they speak his name with tears."

(Percival Phillips in *The Daily Express* and also *The Morning Post*, 22nd August 1917.)

Appendix II

"We had the misfortune to lose our chaplain, Fr Doyle, the other day. He was a real saint and would never leave his men, and it was really marvellous to see him burying dead soldiers under terrible shell fire. He did not know what fear was, and everybody in the battalion, Catholic and Protestant alike, idolised him. I went to Confession to him and received Holy Communion from him a day or two before he was killed, and I feel terribly sorry after him.

"He loved the men and spent every hour of his time looking after them, and when we were having a fairly hot time in the trenches he would bring us up boxes of cigarettes and cheer us up. The men would do anything he asked them, and I am sure we will never get another padre like him. Everybody says that he has earned the V.C. many times over, and I can vouch for it myself from what I have seen him do many a time. He was asked not to go into action with the battalion, but he would not stop behind, and I am confident that no braver or holier man ever fell in battle than he."

(Sergeant T. Flynn, Royal Dublin Fusiliers, from a letter written home and published in *The Irish News*, 29th August 1917.)

Appendix III

The body of the slain priest lay in an unknown grave near the crossroads of Frezenberg; seemingly forgotten. And yet, from his makeshift sepulchre, he was anonymously to influence a book that touched the lives of millions.

First published in 1939, *El Camino* [*The Way*] was quickly to become a spiritual classic, and its author, Father Josemaría Escrivá, was eventually declared a saint.

In the chapter on Mortification, Point 205 reads as follows:

> "We were reading - you and I - the heroically ordinary life of that man of God. And we saw him fight whole months and years (what 'accounts' he kept in his particular examination!) at breakfast time: today he won, tomorrow he was beaten... He noted: 'Didn't take butter... did take butter!'
>
> May you and I too live our 'butter tragedy'."

The subject referred to in this point was Father Willie Doyle. St Josemaría had read a Spanish translation of the life of the Irish Jesuit in 1933 and been greatly affected by it.

He was to write: "I have read quickly the life of Fr Doyle: how well I understand the butter tragedy."

Later in 1938, during the bloodshed of the Spanish Civil War, St Josemaría was reminded of the carnage in which

Fr Willie had exercised his ministry when, in a letter, he wrote the following:

> "I'm quite envious of those on the battlefronts, in spite of everything. It has occurred to me that, if my path were not so clearly marked out, it would be wonderful to outdo Father Doyle."

Father Willie's sacrifice whether of 'butter', or indeed his life, indirectly helped produce at least one canonised saint, to say nothing of the countless others influenced by the spirituality of Opus Dei in their daily struggle for sanctity, albeit not on the fields of battle but at the breakfast table, the work bench, the office...

Sources

Lives of Father Willie Doyle

The direct quotes from Fr Willie Doyle, as indeed the letters referenced, are all taken from the only substantial life on the priest: *Father William Doyle SJ: A Spiritual Study* by Alfred O'Rahilly [Longmans, Green and Co., 1920].

Some years later, published anonymously, there was another biography with some additional information - some suspect that the author was his brother Fr Charles Doyle SJ: *Merry in God: A Life of Father William Doyle SJ* [Longmans, Green and Co., 1939].

There is a chapter entitled: 'Father William Doyle, SJ [1873 -1917]' by Fr James Broderick SJ, in *The Irish Way*, edited by F.J. Sheed [Sheed & Ward, 1932].

In the 1930s *The Irish Messenger* published a number of pamphlets about Fr Willie Doyle:

Father William Doyle, SJ by Rev. Hugh Kelly SJ [*Irish Messenger,* 1928].

Father Willie [Father William Doyle] His worldwide appeal and favours attributed to his intercession [*Irish Messenger*, 1931].

Stories of Father Willie [*Irish Messenger*, 1932].

Works by Father Willie Doyle

Retreats for Working Men: Why not in Ireland? [1909]

Vocations [1913]

Rubrics of the Mass [1914]

Shall I be a Priest? [1915]

Scruples and Their Treatment [manuscript found shortly after his death and published in 1936]

A collection of meditations, prayers and spiritual direction - largely drawn from O'Rahilly's biography: *A Year's Thoughts: Collected from the writings of Father William Doyle, SJ* [Longmans Green and Co., 1922].

In addition, Fr Willie Doyle wrote the foreword and translated from French: *A Man After God's Heart: Life of Father Paul Ginhac, SJ* by Arthur Calvet SJ [R. & T. Washbourne, 1914].

Other references

The 40,000 wartime conversions are cited in: *The Cross on the Sword: Catholic Chaplains in the Forces* by Tom Johnstone & James Hagerty [Geoffrey Chapman, 1996, p. 175].

The references in Appendix III to St Josemaría Escrivá and Father Willie Doyle are taken from: *The Way: A Critical-Historical Edition* prepared by Pedro Rodriguez [Scepter, 2009, pp. 386-388].

J.R.R. Tolkien

Raymond Edwards

JRR Tolkien (1892-1973) is best known as the author of the enduringly popular fantasy novels The Hobbit and The Lord of the Rings, now made into a series of well-regarded blockbuster films. He was also a world-renowned scholar of ancient language, who married the childhood sweetheart who inspired his stories, and was father to four children. He was also a devout Catholic whose faith was central to his writing. This booklet shows how an orphan from Birmingham came to write books that forever changed the way we read.

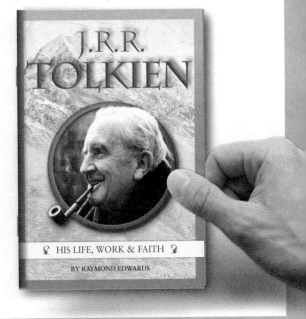

B750   ISBN 978 1 86082 827 0

A world of Catholic reading at your fingertips...

Catholic Faith, Life & Truth for all

www.CTSbooks.org

twitter: @CTSpublishers

facebook.com/CTSpublishers

Catholic Truth Society, Publishers to the Holy See.